I AM NOT INVISIBLE

Reflections on
Meaning & Perspective

MICHAEL HONEY

WalkervillePublishing

Contact: m34h@yahoo.com

ISBN 10# 1514363712
ISBN 13# 9781514363713
Printed in USA

An imprint of Walkerville Publishing Inc.
walkerville.com

Walkerville**Publishing**

TABLE OF CONTENTS

TO

MARY AND ALEX

PREFACE

This is a book about soul. The content is a result of soul seeking both expression and satisfaction. Soul, the mysterious, invisible and restless companion of the human condition. What does soul want? Soul wants to become visible, known, felt, experienced and expressed. Soul seems to have a specific agenda. It wants this and not that. It can sometimes feel as if soul will use any means and opportunity to express itself.

This book is also about both perspective and meaning. What is visible through my perspective and what is invisible to my perspective? Much like soul, meaning can feel as if it is invisible, out of reach and out of sight. Are soul and meaning inherently invisible? Or is it my perspective, my way into and through life, which renders invisible what has always been available and with me all the time?

This book is not thick. This book is concentrated. Each chapter is both a thematic reflection on soul and a reflection of soul. Each chapter is both a standalone piece and an integral part of the collective work. It would seem as if all themes point toward one primary theme. This progression is non-linear. Each theme folds into itself. Each theme wraps around and is the precursor to the next theme. If we consider a theme as an image with some meaning, then herein are many images; and yet there is one image. It is as if this book is a reflection, an expression, an image, of an invisible and restless soul.

INTRODUCTION

A primary theme of this book is perspective. Perspective as more than a way of seeing. I live within what I see. Perspective as more than rose-coloured glasses. Even these rose-coloured glasses have been imagined. These rose-coloured glasses become real and helpful when imagining what, who and where I am and help me to stand slightly beside myself. From this perspective, just off to one side, I imagine peering into myself and into the world in which I live: a world I have created. Any meaning uncovered in our lives is a function of perspective. Within our lives we encounter things that have the quality of being invisible. I can feel something there, I can sense something there, but I cannot directly perceive what 'it' is. Any search for meaning, or any desire to create meaning, will draw one towards the boundaries of one's perspective, towards the invisible. I can feel the invisible. The invisible can rattle around within me.

This book also contains perspectives related to seeking to return the invisible into the visible, to discovering something meaningful inside of what feels like nothing more than a fantasy. Fantasy can also be a new perspective seeking to come into being within us. In this perspective, fantasy is more than make-believe, more than intention, and more than attraction. Fantasy is the perspective of soul and therefore the place of transformation between the invisible and the visible, between the seen and the unseen, between what is meaningless and what can be meaningful.

The book's other primary theme is meaning. What is meaning? Where is meaning? What does meaning feel like? Why do I seek meaning? Is meaning the language and longing of soul?

We can often only understand a meaningful pattern when reviewing what we have done after it has happened. Something meaningful may be happening even when we do not see any meaning. How can we also begin to see, feel or begin to trust that something meaningful is happening at any given moment, even if this meaning is not felt and visible?

The motivation for this book is that various parts of my soul were seeking to become visible, known, felt, experienced and expressed. Here I will repeat the working image for soul which will be used throughout the book. Soul is the mysterious, invisible and restless companion of the human condition. Contained within any personal experience is a common human collective experience. This book has been written with this conviction: what has been helpful and meaningful for me and my soul may also be helpful and meaningful for you and your soul.

IN THE
BEGINNING

A challenge contained within the beginning of any new process is waiting for the scheduled starting time and date. Then it will begin. Right here and now there is only waiting and anticipation. The waiting and anticipation are more than a prelude. These feelings signal that a new process is already living and moving within you. A new job, a new place to live, a new relationship begin to take shape within you and your imagination before the scheduled starting time and date. In this sense, a beginning is also a continuation and intensification of what has already been happening. The images within this reflection relate to 'something,' 'nothing' and the creative impulse of soul.

Thus it begins. Seemingly creating something out of nothing. The coming into being of something that did not exist before today. I am full of something that has a life in me, and that will have a life of its own. At this early stage of the process, I feel pregnant, full, distended, wishing that whatever has been growing and taking shape will move from the inside to the outside, from sheltered gestation, to a fragile unique separate existence. This fragile, unique, and separate existence is part me yet also feels as if it is not part of me. I feel as if I am unable to create on my own. It feels as if there is a seemingly silent partner, or better, seemingly silent partners, who begin to inform this life-building creation process. The creation of something out of nothing is a collaboration of some-things. This movement to express something is a combination, a collaboration, a concentration of something working within something.

It is important to ask, which concepts inform this work? Which theories determine what is observed and what is brightened? Even this previous sentence is loaded with implications, concepts and theories. The process of questioning the foundations of a thesis, of a seemingly personal expression, can be an infinite regression which can literally reduce everything into nothing, into nothing but 'my opinion', into a blank page. Then there is no place to start for each place is every place such that every place is nowhere. There is no sense of meaning for a reader or author of a blank page, of blank pages, of empty pages, of pages devoid of fantasy, mystery, imagination, and landscape. Blank pages, devoid of opinion, imagination and perspective are nothing. What follows is fantasy, imagination, alive with implications, concepts and theories. What follows, and what has already been stated, is something.

This book is personal in that it flows from my life experience. This is something of me. On another level this book is simply something. It now is. The process of this coming into being was neither an easy process, nor a short-term process. The process of this coming into being was both enjoyable and arduous. This is what soul wanted. The end result was something: something which feels meaningful. Meaninglessness is related to nothingness, sameness, lack of distinction and lack of differentiation. Meaning can begin to be found in recognising separateness, discreetness, in sticking with the image, in working to create something from what feels like nothing, by being in-relation-to something.

THE CENTER OF
GRAVITY OF BEING

In speaking about the beginning of the universe, even of my own beginning, it is possible to say that something was created from nothing. There seems to be something which is the source of all that exists. Theologically, psychologically, scientifically before any beginning there is darkness. Then there is light. Then there are shadows. When reflecting on the beginning of the universe and within each new beginning within my life, how can I find that solid stable place which is at home in the darkness, light, shadows and continuous movement of life? The images of home, soul and center of gravity of being are but three answers to this question.

IN THE BEGINNING WAS DARKNESS.

AT THE MOMENT BEFORE ALL CONCEPTION,

THERE WAS DARKNESS, THEN THERE WAS LIGHT.

EACH ITERATIVE RETURN, ORBITS THE CREATIVE DARKNESS,

WHICH IS THE CONSTANT SOURCE OF LIFE.

EACH ITERATIVE RETURN IS A RETURNING TOWARDS THE BEGINNING,

A RETURNING TOWARDS THE INVISIBLE, A RETURNING TOWARDS THAT

WHICH SEEMS INDESTRUCTIBLE.

THE CENTER OF GRAVITY OF BEING.

BEYOND WHICH IS THE SENSE OF NOTHING, BEYOND WHICH IS THE

MOMENT BEFORE.

A RETURNING BEYOND THE VALLEY OF THE SHADOW OF DEATH.

A RETURNING INSIDE THE VALLEY OF THE SHADOW OF LIFE,

WHERE ONE CAN LIVE IN THE LIGHT OF DARKNESS,

WHERE ONE CAN LIVE IN THE LIGHT WHICH IS DARKNESS,

WHERE ONE CAN LIVE WITH THE LIGHT THAT IS AT HOME IN DARKNESS.

AS EXPERIENCE FLOWS, AS THOUGHTS FLOW, AS FEELINGS FLOW, AS WORDS

FLOW, AS IMAGES FLOW, THERE IS RECONCILIATION, GENERATING DEGREES

OF FREEDOM OF MOVEMENT.

BEYOND THE POTENTIAL OF THE ALMOST, AND THE POSSIBILITY OF

THE INVISIBLE,

INSIDE THE CENTER OF GRAVITY OF BEING,

THERE IS A RETURNING TO AN EXPERIENCE OF BEING LIVED WITHIN.

THIS IS WHERE SOUL IS, THIS IS WHERE HOME IS.

Seeking to find one's place, not only within day-to-day life, but within the limitlessness of the universe can be frightening. In the beginning was darkness; then there was light. I can imagine a big bang or some divine event bringing the universe into being, light from darkness, something from nothing. What is my place in this universe? It can make me feel as if I am nothing, in relation to all that exists, and therefore meaningless.

Having studied physics, the question of my place in the universe was both fascinating and terrifying. According to physics anything with mass, such as you and I, has a center of mass. My center of mass is my physical point of balance. Balanced on this point I do not feel pushed or pulled in any particular direction by gravity. This is a place of stability. Grounded. My physical center within me. A balanced place of reference. I can translate the center of gravity of mass psychologically and begin to imagine a center of gravity of being. How can I begin to find the center of gravity of my being? How much of this search is a spiritual process and how much of this exploration is a psychological process? Either way, by discovering some image, or experience of my center of gravity of being, I also locate something which feels secure and indestructible. It is always there. When I wonder off, away from this center, it remains the stable solid place I can return to and be welcomed home. My center of gravity of being has always been with me, and will continue to be with me. I can even imagine that my center of gravity of being is where soul finds its home. Beginning to have an internal sense of both soul and home will carry with it a sense of meaning and be an internal center towards which all of me can gravitate and feel grounded.

THE PLACE
OF CREATION

Where is our internal place of creation? What is happening within this internal place? It is possible to say that I am being moved or that I feel inspired. These may well be good metaphors to describe the process of personal creativity. Other times the process of personal creativity, be it a poem, song, or cooking can feel as if this animation of personal creativity has temporarily arrived and taken up residence within me. This creative animation can feel as if it is something or someone distinct from me has arrived for a visit to work something out though me. Other times there is a clear sense that we are working together to create something new. Who is this creative other I feel within me? This may well be the felt presence of soul at work.

And there he sits, writing; contemplating what will come into being between ink and paper. As he writes he considers what a cool metaphor "coming into being between ink and paper" is. Simultaneously grasping and not grasping his spontaneous insight is exciting for him. It is cool to be aware when such things happen. It is frustrating to be unable to keep hold of and claim full ownership of this simple beauty.

Where does this come from? He thinks it is me. Yet in the end, I have the same experience as him, yet in reverse, because I know it is not me, not him, not entirely a sum of us. He knows I am here and often tries to watch me, in the same manner I watch him. When he hears me going on like this, he will quietly and gently stand beside me. There is a mutual acknowledgment of knowing and being known, but then we each go our own way, neither of us able to hold for very long this symbiotic mutual affliction of seeing by being seen, of knowing by being known, of being mutually creative, of simply seeing what happens within the interaction, of using all our resources to give birth to something new. Together we discover each outcome of effort. Together we re-learn the properties of our discovery materials. Together we play.

The mystery is knowing I am writing this, of being aware I am having an experience of this, of watching the page fill with what comes into being between ink and paper. It is never the same. Sometimes I have not thought the words, and am conscious of seeing the words unfold before I recognize them. Other times I feel the elusive one watching me and then whisper something to someone. Then the little shit shies away, gone as soon as I try to say hello. I will need to reread what I have just written yet have a sense I will save everything because I am writing with 'one of those feelings' where the pen moves, the words flow, like a river without source, a wind without direction, from a place like home but without an address.

Learning not to seek the address, the location on the map, is part of the learning process. Only then do I imagine home as a perspective rather than a specific place. This includes seeking the place where I reside, a comfortable dwelling where each room is a place I can call home. There seems to be more than just 'me' inside my home. Within this perspective, there is a place to build beauty and a place to watch beauty flow. Within this perspective, I discover a place of feeling lived within, no matter the current or future weather forecast. The rain washes, the snow slows everything down, I can discover things in lightning, while thunder shakes things free. The beauty of home may last through the seasons, or the beauty of home may undo itself when forces tip out of balance, and this creation is unable to sustain itself.

Sometimes within the search for meaning, the focus on the search itself can obscure or obstruct from view anything meaningful. The "full on" search for meaning can unleash a sense of meaninglessness. In looking so very hard for something, I may find nothing. Learning not to look for the address of meaning, for its location on a map, is part of the process. This includes a place to build beauty and to watch beauty flow. Beauty is a collaboration. A collaboration between some things and some ones, as if something or someone moves within and through me as I create. Inside of beauty I can find a comfortable place of being lived within. Together we can create, play and enjoy. Discovering where there is a place of being lived within, the center of gravity of being, an internal place of beauty, can be meaningful.

TIC, TOC, SOUL

There are macro components of daily life within us influencing how we live each day. These daily components are so intertwined within our being they can easily become overlooked and accepted as a normal part of daily life. What is easier to grasp and name are the effects of such components. The price of gas and taxes are too high. I want to make more money. I wish I could afford better clothes, a newer car, or to go someplace warm during the winter. To speak about money, or lack thereof, is to speak about the effect of the economy. This synthetic creation runs on money, time and soul, affecting what I do and who I am. If only I could win the lottery. This may provide me more money but can money ransom and heal my soul?

The economy has become the global god, idol, the modern myth. In various ways, we have all embarked on this mythical journey, which promises some sense of satisfaction, fulfilling a need, or desire, when consuming this myth's products. We trade time for money, money for merchandise. A 'good deal' is considered a 'fair trade'.

In the satisfaction that derives from acquisitions, the negative consequences of the economy on animate and inanimate objects are often ignored. The impact of the economy on everything visible and invisible. The economy has become omnipresent, seeking omnipotence, commanding a total commitment of doing, a total commitment of being. What am I doing within 'the economy'? What is 'the economy' doing to me?

I AM SELLING MY TIME FOR MONEY.

I AM TRADING MY TIME FOR MONEY.

I AM SELLING AND TRADING MYSELF FOR MONEY.

I SELL MY SOUL, PIECE BY PIECE, HOUR BY HOUR.

THEN I PURCHASE INSIDE THE ECONOMY, LOCAL OR GLOBAL.

I SACRIFICE MYSELF, TO MAKE MONEY, TO SPEND MY MONEY, TO GET WHAT I WANT OR NEED.

EACH PIECE OF SOUL GONE, SACRIFICED TO THE GODS, SACRIFICED EVEN TO THE HOLY TRINITY OF FOOD, CLOTHING AND SHELTER.

I LAY MYSELF TO WASTE. I SACRIFICE SLEEP. I GO TO WORK IN DANGEROUS WEATHER.

I GO TO WORK FATIGUED WITH ILLNESS — TO TRADE MY TIME FOR MONEY.

LOOK AROUND ON THE SIDEWALKS, LOOK AROUND ON THE SUBWAY, LOOK INTO THE CAR BESIDE,

WE ARE IN SERVICE TO KRONOS.

KRONOS, THE SACRIFICIAL GOD OF THE ECONOMY.

KRONOS DEMANDS A CONTINUOUS SACRIFICE OF SELF.

A LIVING SACRIFICE.

CONTINUOUSLY GIVING, CONTINUOUSLY MOVING, TO THE TICK-TICK-TICK OF KRONOS.

AS THE MARROW IS SUCKED FROM BONES,

AS MUSCLES TIGHTEN WITH STRESS,

THE BEAT GOES ON,

AND THE BEAT GOES ON.

THE DAILY GRIND, THE DAILY GRIND, THE DAILY GRIND.

BEING SLOWLY GROUND INTO DUST,

SO THAT IT IS I WHO AM BLOWING IN THE WIND.

AS I MOVE UP THE MONEY LADDER,

WHAT OF ME IS LEFT STANDING ON THE GROUND?

ARE THESE MY FEET?

THEY ARE NOT THE FEET I REMEMBER.

THE FEET WALKING WITH CURIOSITY,

SEEMING TO HAVE A MIND OF THEIR OWN,

MOVING ME FROM ADVENTURE TO ADVENTURE.

OR WALKING IN THE GARDEN IN THE COOL OF THE EVENING,

GROUNDED.

NOW MY FEET STEP TO THE BEAT OF KRONOS,

TO WHOM I SELL MY SOUL,

PIECE BY PIECE,

TICK TOCK SOUL.

MY SOUL IS NOT FOR SALE.

MY SOUL IS NOT DISPOSABLE.

MY SOUL IS NOT RECYCLABLE.

MY SOUL IS FOR ME.

MY SOUL IS FOR YOU.

NO MONEY REQUIRED.

NON-ECONOMIC.

One of the challenges with finding meaning is contained within the collective context of daily life. I can be at church, or therapy, having good discussions with friends and family, reading a book, or even taking a course at a university entitled: "The Meaning of Life" (I did this!). I can gain something from each of these experiences. Such insights might not hold, and can easily fade. It might be simple for me to conclude that there is something within me that truly does not want to have and hold onto anything meaningful. This can even cause me to wonder if there is anything of lasting value and meaning. This place is where awareness of how the collective cultural and historical context might be effecting my search and location of meaning. A personal cultural and historical context, when and where I am living, may well be contained within something I encounter every day. A something I do not find meaningful. A something more than able to strip away any sense of meaning within my grasp. I exist within an economic system wherein I sell and trade my time for money. Even on Sundays. The current economic system requires a continual sacrifice. A living sacrifice. I sell myself, I sell my soul, I sell my center of gravity hour by hour. And yet, there is likely nothing amiss with my search for meaning. The barriers into meaning are both collective and personal. Collective barriers into meaning can be most harmful when they remain invisible.

ECONOMICS OF A PLACE
CALLED HOME

How much does your ranking within the economy, your income, the money you receive for the time you spend working, have an influence on where you live and call home? Is home comfortable and nourishing? Is home where I can easily imagine living for another five or ten years? Is home defined by what I can currently afford? As soon as I get a raise I am going to move to a new and better neighborhood. The economy will have an influence on your internal sense of home as it determines the physical place you call home. More money can be helpful for breathing easier and lessening worry about the bills. At the same time, money is not a cure-all for any sense of personal discontent. The human soul seems to be a restless companion of the human condition. The human soul is not easily satisfied and soul satisfaction requires more than money.

A city exists within its own cultural context, offering unique sources of global and local options. Am I more of an urban, in-the-city type of person, living near a large park, in a neighbourhood with street shopping accessible on foot? In this scenario, my car can remain parked for days on end. There is much walking, people on the streets and recognizable faces. The sidewalks know these feet. Living close to the ground within some part of the inner city can also be more expensive than the suburbs. Am I more of a suburban type living near spaces covered in concrete and asphalt? All or most of my suburban shopping, errands and activities involve driving to and fro. I get into and out of my car. The asphalt knows my tires. The rubber tires insulate me from my surroundings. Insulate me from being grounded onto and into a specific geography of the place I call home. On the road and ungrounded. On the move in my car because my neighbourhood was designed more for cars than for me and my feet.

The social and historical population shift from inner cities to the suburbs during the 1950's – 1980's is often associated with a desire of so-called middle class families to move away from inner urban decay. What had once been the vibrant inner city was seen as crumbling and undesirable. Since 1990, most inner cities have experienced re-population and revitalization movements. Inner city urban areas continue to grow, as do the suburbs. There also seems to be a shift in the economic demographics of the inner and outer city. Once, the so-called comfortable middle class was able to afford a move out of the inner city to the spacious lands of the outer city. The so-called comfortable middle class is now moving back into the inner city, repopulating the heart. Work is closer to home for those who can afford this option. Housing costs though, are lower in the suburbs. I live in the suburbs because it is affordable. I drive to the city for work, resulting in less time in my home. The suburbs may have once promised the hope of a new and better way of life.

Since 1990, suburban areas have become the place that is affordable enough for me to call my own. I live here because this is what I can afford. This is mine. My suburban home has become a place of survival, month to month, as long as my job is not declared redundant. I live in an ungrounded place full of frustrated dreams, with the associated stress humming below the surface. In this place where is my local and where is my global? Where is my house, my home, because I turned into the wrong driveway last night? Rather than recognize familiar faces while out for a walk, instead I see familiar faces waiting impatiently in the big box store checkout line.

In the 1990's the changes taking place between the urban and suburban began to be theologized. What is the theological meaning of these social and economic changes? Any Christian theology inevitably speaks to a personal need to be saved from some sort of sinfulness, not only from actions, but also at the deepest core of my soul. Yet in the daily grind, me and my soul are busy, working to survive within the economy. Even if I am not in it only for the money, I am working to ensure I have food, clothing and shelter and perhaps some savings. I am working towards a place where I need not worry about money, towards a place where I can breathe easier. I am not interested in a theology telling me I am inherently broken. I may feel broken, but certainly I was not born broken. What is it, then, that has broken within me, continues to break me to pieces, slowly grinding me into dust? What existing theory, system, or perspective is ruling the lives of all people?

The economy. The economy demands a continuous living sacrifice. The sacrifice of my time for money so that I am may afford to live in the world of this synthetic god.

How do I reconcile my soul with economy? How do I keep and hold myself together in the presence of this god, this synthetic divine other? I may choose to theologize that I feel broken because I was born broken. I am born broken because two people ate the fruit of a specific tree. Theologically reconciling myself and my brokenness with a part of my soul may feel better and some part of me may breathe easier. In this theological process I also call on a large amount of other theological and psychological implications regarding me and my soul. It may not be long before I begin to feel broken again and to have the feeling that something is trying to break me. I may project this re-emergence of a deep-rooted sense of brokenness as bad faith or as attacks of fallen angels. Neither response sees far enough through and far enough into what is happening.

Another perspective is that I am born unbroken. I feel broken simply because that is how I feel. What image brings this feeling? This feeling that something is not right, that there is a crack in the system. I may feel so broken it appears I am falling apart, going to pieces. I can also feel broken because something is working against my soul, against my image, slowly tearing me apart, piece by piece. Slowly grinding me into dust, day by day. This something is synthetic, man-made, and yet has the capacity of a god or demon to break me, grind me, and dehumanize me. The economy is a human invention yet the scope and reach of its effect on individual lives has become godlike, impersonal, and imminent. The economy has become a collective power of both the conscious and the unconscious. I may not be able to physically remove myself from the economy but I may begin to distill something of my soul's dissatisfaction and begin to put myself back together again. Separating out what my soul does not want.

In 1990, I set in search of a new and relevant way to theologize the role of the church vis. the city. I was also seeking a new theology, a new 'ology'. I found this new 'ology' within psychology. A way of looking at and looking into me, people, places and things. A new perspective. What seems to be more important now is the ability to look at and into the larger constructs influencing my life day-by-day and hour-by-hour, such as the economy. At this point, 'ologies' no longer seem separate and self-contained. It is no longer theology versus psychology. Each folds into the other. Each relies on the other for continued existence. Theology and psychology each speak to something such as brokenness, and offer perspectives of healing. Perspectives of soul. No matter where I live, within the inner or the outer, grounded or ungrounded, there will always be something which feels broken, in need of some form of restoration. Soul. There is a soul which can enjoy the many wonderful offerings of life, and there is a soul which is never quite satisfied with the here and now. Soul: the restless companion of the human condition.

Sometimes there is only a feeling. A feeling seemingly important. A feeling you have learned, telling you that there is something inside that wants out, something inside that wants expression. Often something wants out through writing, as when I was writing about the urban and suburban, and the economy. Other times a walk helps shake things free. Or a good nap settles the scattered pieces into some recognisable image. Each thing that wants out can seek a different vehicle of expression. Each thing that wants out might not fully reveal itself until the end of the process, as if the meaning finding expression, the vehicle of expression, and the perseverance to stick with it are all part and parcel of the same package. Over and over, there does not appear to be any quick fix, or easy way around to finding or expressing trust in the insistence of soul. The challenge is to move any 'ology' away from being 'the way'. A servant and not a master. It seems any 'ology' is a way into, a way through, and a way back, a vehicle providing some satisfaction to the restless companion of the human condition. The satisfaction of mystery, imagination, meaning, and the flame of distillation.

THE RATTLE
IN OUR SHADOW

In the beginning is darkness. Then there is light. Then there are shadows. We can be afraid of the dark. We can be afraid of what is lurking in the shadows. The shadow, a place in-between the beginning and what comes next. Shadow, a mixture of the infinite depth of darkness and the in your face intensity of light. The shadow of a tree can offer welcome shade on a hot summer day. The same shadow can conceal a nasty crack in the sidewalk when out for a walk after sunset. Psychologically, the human shadow can have similar characteristics. Rather than imagine what is hiding or lurking in the shadows, it may be better to ask what has been hidden within the shadow. If I have hidden part of me away, have I not also hidden away part of my soul? Hidden away for whatever the reason. Every once in a while something from within the shadow can rattle for attention because it is time for it to come home.

What is it that begins to rattle, rattle, rattle within us? We can hear and feel the vibration of these rattles. We seek its source. It cannot be seen because it is still invisible. It exists because I know it is there. It rattles. The vibration and the noise of the rattle keep me awake at night. The vibration and the noise continue to call out for recognition. That annoying rattle feels like a song that never ends. That annoying rattle begins to resonate uncomfortably inside my bones.

What is the source of this rattle? I want to know. I want to make it stop. I wonder if this rattle is the symptom or the disease. Now I'm curious. This rattle certainly has my attention. It has vibrated me to attention. This at least is a beginning.

Perhaps this rattling for attention is something I have chosen to ignore, or left behind on my last personal iteration? Perhaps I left this behind, hoping never to see it again. Rather than reuse and recycle, I repress. How can I begin to pay attention and tune into whatever it is I have somehow learned to ignore, to push aside, to forget, to leave behind, to turn invisible? What is it that I have repressed? What are those parts of me, which for some reason are too difficult to continue to leave out in the open, out there, out here, right now, as a visible part of me? What is it that I have hidden in the shadows, within my own shadow?

It is me, parts of me.

Sometimes one or more parts of me decide it is time to return. This part of me wants to return from exile. This part of me makes some noise because it wants to return home and once again be visible. Now is the time. This is the annoying rattle speaking to me across my imaginal boundary. The imaginal boundary of me, and not me. The boundary is imaginal because me, and not me, are both me. As I begin to pay attention to the rattle I may begin to attune, to tune into myself. The location of this rattle, the so-called shadow, sounds mysterious, feels invisible and can seem to have something of a "dark, dead-end back alley at night" vibe. This is not a place full of straight-ahead exits, or side exits. There is only one way in and one way out. The way in is the way out. The way out is the way in. I am the way.

There is something within my shadow that begins to rattle and calls to me from time to time, reminding me that it is there. I am here. Reminding me that some part of me would like to return home from this shadowy place of exile. Through attention and attunement I have found my way both to the rattle and to its source. I have found a part of me speaking from the exile of shadows. Perhaps my soul will be restless as long as there are parts of me rattling within the shadows of exile. Perhaps my restless soul and the soles of my restless feet seek to return me to me, turning my invisible back into the visible.

When we find meaning, when we find something meaningful within the shadow, what is it we have found? Perhaps something of ourselves. Something of ourselves which has been in exile. Something which we have, for whatever reason, exiled into the shadows of consciousness. There seems to be more soul food than fear to be found within the shadow. The rattle in our shadow can be meaningful, vibrating us to attention, attuning us to all of who we always have been.

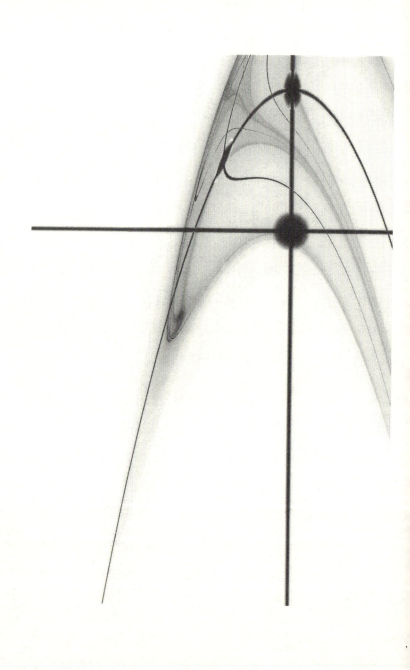

ITERATIONS
OF PSYCHE

It can be said that the experience of life is not about the destination, rather life is about the journey. What is the implied meaning contained within saying life is about the journey? It is difficult to find anyone who can provide a satisfactory answer to this question. Does not the word journey imply a beginning, middle and end, a destination? Focusing on a journey towards a destination can have a linear feel. I am incrementally moving from point A to point B as if I know where point B is and as if point B will be my place of recovery and satisfaction. It may be that life is about iterations. Iterations of self, soul and psyche. Each new personal iteration lands me into a place containing something unanticipated. My personal shit is a part of each iteration. Each iteration is an expression of what soul wants. Getting down and dirty with my own shit will help keep the landing area from being an overly messy experience.

I have thought about iterations, ie: personal iterations over the years. Usually thinking about making due with what I have at the time, and then paying attention for new variables to account and fold into the next iteration. This would be paying attention for the variables that fit and for the variables that do not seem to fit and yet somehow belong within my $(n+1)$ iterative process. Output is taken as input. Seems simple enough. Not very complex. Just feed all the good shit back into the equation of me.

Alongside the good shit, there is a certain amount of naturally occurring radioactivity within a system which would seem to be readily absorbed by the system, becoming simply one of the many nested variables. This naturally occurring radioactivity is always available within a system, forming a standard part of the $(n+1)$ iterating system.

There are variables that appear to be hiding, and variables that seem easy to ignore and leave behind. These variables are not integrated into the next personal iteration. These variables sit, waiting for their seat on the next $(n+1)$ iterative ride. As they wait, they begin to rot. As they rot they become radioactive, contaminating their surroundings. This is not naturally occurring radiation but rather synthetic radiation. The danger is not contained within the mere presence of radioactivity. The danger is folded within the amount and type of personal synthetic radiation allowed to accumulate within the overall process. Personal radioactivity is a marker announcing where it is during any $(n+1)$ iteration. In announcing its presence within the process, it also attracts attention. Each iteration is the end result of choices I have made. Choices I make for whatever reason. Choices which end up moving me. I choose this, not that. Is there choice in having a choice? I take a stand, make a choice and I end up feeling as if I am neither here nor there.

Maybe the dangerous accumulation of synthetic radioactivity is simply a result of where I have squatted and had a shit the last time through the process, and chose to not scoop up after myself. This shit was left as waste product, not picked up, and not fed back into the input of the next $(n+1)$ iteration. The new me. Interesting property of this shit – this shit will strange attract to itself, becoming consequential to the outcome of the current plus one iteration. Said another way, this shit contains a nested strange attractor in-relation-to itself and to the overall system process. Meaning: after enough iterations there will be enough shit. Enough of my shit that I can no longer walk by the steaming pile, unaware that it is there, nor ignoring that it is part of me. Enough of my shit that all I can do is iterate directly into my steaming pile and carry some shit off and away with me and into the next iteration.

It would seem that my shit has an inherent self-management system. My steaming pile of synthetic radioactive shit can become smaller as I work through it. A little smaller with each iteration. Then small enough that I can choose to ignore my shit, again, or I can choose to keep walking through my own shit, becoming one with these old parts of me, transforming the old output into new input. I can clean myself up by cleaning up after myself. And at least feeling shit free while I am in that wonderful mysterious place between (n) and (n+1).

Looking for meaning and trying to be aware of where meaning is, will bring with it some sort of change as a part of the process. Any given change may be wonderfully welcome or may be unconsciously ignored, repressed. Any given change will initiate some form of personal iteration. This may be a small change and a small iteration. Something feels a little bit different. This may be a large change, and a large iteration. Everything old feels as new again. Either way it will be important, it will be meaningful, to learn to be able to notice, pay attention, to tune into what I carry with me and the shit I leave behind with each iteration. What is left behind within each personal iteration, either consciously or unconsciously, will begin to dampen and cast a shadow upon any sense of wellbeing and meaning. I can frustrate my own sense of wellbeing, my own sense of meaning, through the process I use to adapt to personal change. You will not need to look long and hard to find your 'shit', your 'shit' will find you.

GOD, CONSCIOUSNESS & ATOMS

Pierre Teilhard de Chardin was schooled in theology, philosophy, paleontology and geology, writing in the early 1900's. He was living life through more than one perspective. These viewpoints allowed him to learn from what he found within the dust of the earth and to speculate about the origins and meaning of the dust on his hands. To what extent is the universe and all of life the result of a big bang and to what extent is the universe and all of life the result of some divine event? For Teilhard de Chardin the answer seems to be a bit of both. The big bang, and the development and meaning of human conscious existence are intertwined for this author. Consciousness gives us an awareness of soul. We can then also say that the big bang and soul are intertwined for Teilhard de Chardin. You cannot have one without the other. Teilhard de Chardin offers what may be called a Christian answer to this question, and you may well find that his perspective is a welcome departure from the common Christian perspective.

Theologian Pierre Teilhard de Chardin was seized by theological images and meanings, and he did his best to express these in words so other people might see what he was seeing, and be moved by what was moving in him. Within his texts, there is more than classical Christian theology of a human and earth-centered history, and a human and earth-centered encounter with a Christian God. This included the movement of humans, on earth, over a few thousand years, into two covenants with God. For Teilhard de Chardin, it seemed the entire universe is in view, the entire universe is in motion, with a particular purpose. Teilhard de Chardin seems to be searching for a language and a theology which had room for, and could be meaningful, not only within the context of human history on earth, but also within the context of the entire history of the universe, including each distinct atom.

Teilhard de Chardin appears to re-image theology, bringing into view a vision of the history of the universe in relation to consciousness. This is a new vision, a transformation of the invisible to the visible, a new perspective. Teilhard de Chardin seemed to imagine a coming into being and a coming into consciousness as a basic property of all life, of the entire universe. He is speaking of a universal evolution. This is much more than a survival of the fittest evolution. It may be better to speak of a progression, or a movement, within a particular direction of every atom and of all of life. The universe is the "all" of life. Humans are one part of this universe. Teilhard de Chardin seems to be speaking mostly of an ongoing, since the beginning of time, evolution of consciousness, with humans seemingly the best example of this evolution of consciousness. One of the basic things that can be learned from biology is that life feeds upon life. The complexity of any organism requires a continuous input of energy. Thus all living things eat in some way. Molecules feeding on molecules is insufficient to produce or to sustain life and the universe we have come to know. Entropy will ensure this is so.

My undergraduate studies were in physics. I particularly enjoyed nuclear physics and stellar evolution. Through equations I was – and am still – able to imagine, to see, the infinite expanse of the universe, the inner workings of atomic particles, the curvature of space and time, and the infinite nothingness of a black hole. This is both wonderful and terrifying. Theologically, it has never been enough to say 'God created the universe' and 'God has acted in human history.' If what I have come to see and understand through physics has any connection to objective truth, to the 'way things really are', then the standard creation and salvation stories speak only to part of me, and only a part of the universe within which I live, move and write. Even 'omnipresent' is not sufficient to bridge this gap of perspective. Omnipresent where? On earth? In my life, in your life? What about the entire arc of universal, earth and human history? What about the electrons in my cells, and the 'uncertainty' of how the electron in one of my cells is going to behave at any given time?

At this point in our journey, we arrive at the other side of this story. By being able to imagine, to see the infinite expanse of the universe, the inner workings of atomic particles, the curvature of space and time, and the infinite nothingness of a black hole, I discovered the physical laws were able to aptly describe what did and is happening. Physical laws were holding all things together in some way. I was also beginning to see that the physical laws do not appear to be functioning independently of anything or anyone else. There is enough 'uncertainty' within any measurement, within the roots of atomic structure, that it seems as if physical laws are not self-sufficient. There appears to be something holding the root structure of me, the entire universe, and the physical laws together. It is as if there remains something invisible working within the universe, the physical laws and human history. Within Teilhard de Chardin's focus there seems to be the entire arc of the universe's history from a human perspective. What is happening now in human history, yet when holding the massive expanse of time and space and the universe in mind, what has always been happening that has brought us to this point? What has happened over the long duration of the universe is that humans have come into being with a certain consciousness, which allows us to be aware of that which can be called the invisible. This coming into being with a certain consciousness is not the result of some random process. What is being described, at the root level, is not an autonomous process of change, of inanimate matter randomly reconfigured, of impersonal physical laws, and therefore meaningless, randomly generating the place where we now stand in history, where we come to conclusions about the phenomena of the universe, of man, of God, and of what has been God's part in this universal process. The wonders of what has been, and continues to be have always been available within the universe since the beginning. The ability to recognise, to see, and to consciously participate in the beauty and wonder of human existence is the result of both human history and the history of the universe. There seems to be something within the very fabric of space and time and matter that, given enough duration, eventually brings into being reflective consciousness, and this reflective consciousness can come into a direct awareness and relationship with the invisible. There is something with a direction. As such, the universe can be said to be friendly and even meaningful. The dust and atoms of the universe are somehow wired with a particular direction and purpose.

Teilhard de Chardin is speaking about perspectives, ie: perspectives of phenomena. A perspective, a new way of imagining and describing, may be something new, yet the phenomenon tends to be the same, always available, at any time. A change in perspective can change the universe. A change in perspective can change the invisible into the visible.

A change in perspective can lead to a new point of view regarding the universe, as it did for Teilhard de Chardin. His inherited theological universe seems to have become too small for him. Teilhard de Chardin seems to have been concerned with making sense of the billions of years of earth history and of the billions of years of universe history. The theology he inherited wasn't meaningful enough for him. Teilhard de Chardin required an image of God involved within the entire history of the universe and within every atom of the universe. Teilhard de Chardin was searching for a more meaningful theology. And his theology grappled with the root of consciousness itself. The consciousness reading this book and the consciousness which ponders the meaning of life.

In some sense this is a return to the age-old question: "Is the universe a friendly place?" and then tweaks the question to, "How can the universe be a meaningful place, a place where reflective consciousness is not some random occurrence?" Reflective consciousness is somehow folded into the very structure of space and time and atoms. This is a definite change in theological perspective. Teilhard de Chardin is speaking about perspectives, perspectives of phenomena, of what is happening, or what has always been happening yet has remained concealed, due to a perspective. The universe can be the result of a big bang or the result of some divine event. Either way, it is. Within Teilhard de Chardin's personal theological struggle and search for meaning, the universe becomes meaningful, with a direction and a purpose. Imagine that. The personal meaning I uncover may be larger than my life and me, and helpful to other people within their search for meaning.

IMAGINAL
BOUNDARIES

It is not the drop that slips into the ocean but the ocean that slips into the drop.

This can be a comforting phrase. In saying this phrase I affirm that I belong to something much larger than myself. The ocean is almost endless, deep, dark below the surface and full of mysterious life. The ocean and the drop are one and the same. I can imagine being comforted through finding a home within this immense self-same collective. The ocean and the drop are vastly different in size. I can imagine being afraid of being swallowed whole and assimilated into an undifferentiated collective. What happens to me in this process? Is the ocean slipping into the drop the end of me or the beginning of my next personal iteration? The challenge here for soul is maintaining its specific personal agenda when in relationship to a collective influence.

IT IS NOT THE DROP THAT SLIPS INTO THE OCEAN BUT THE OCEAN
THE SLIPS INTO THE DROP.

OH HOW I DISLIKE THIS PHASE. ALL SO WARM AND FUZZY
AND INCOMPLETE.

THIS PHRASE HAS BEEN WEIGHED, MEASURED, INTUITED, EXPERIENCED
AND FOUND TO BE INSUFFICIENT AND UNSATISFACTORY.

THIS TOO SHALL BE ASSIMILATED.

FOR THE OCEAN ALSO 'SLIPS INTO' AND IS EASILY ABSORBED.

THE OCEAN AND DROP SLIP INTO THE EARTH.

THE EARTH AND OCEAN AND DROP SLIP INTO THE SOLAR SYSTEM.

THE SOLAR SYSTEM AND EARTH AND OCEAN AND DROP SLIP INTO
THE COSMOS.

AS I SLIP AGAIN THERE IS A 'THUD,' FOR AS I SLIP AGAIN,

I SLIP INTO AN IMAGINAL BOUNDARY.

THIS FAR AND NO FURTHER.

YES, METAPHOR.

ALL ARE METAPHORS OF ABSORPTION.

ALL ARE METAPHORS, OF MERGER, OF PAYING ATTENTION,
OF ATTUNEMENT, OF BEING IN TUNE WITH.

ALL ARE METAPHORS OF THE SUBTLE DEPENDING OF PERSPECTIVE
THROUGH THE REMOVAL OF THE DISTINCTION OF DISCREETNESS.

ALL ARE METAPHORS OF THE REMOVAL OF TIME AND SPACE THROUGH
RECONCILIATION.

I AM THE VEHICLE OF RECONCILIATION.

I AM THE POINT OF RECONCILIATION BETWEEN MYSELF AND WHAT
MY SOUL DESIRES.

I FOLLOW MYSELF HOME AND I SLIP INTO MYSELF BECAUSE

I AM THE OCEAN.

AND THIS TOO SHALL SLIP.

*Every once in a while it is possible to encounter a phrase some,
or even most people find helpful within their search for meaning. This phrase can irritate you to no end, anger you, frustrate you, rattle around within you, or it may not ring true in
your soul. Your response, such as my response to: 'It is not the
drop that slips into the ocean but the ocean that slips into the
drop,' can help you define something of your sense of meaning
in direct contrast to a clear response of no, that is not for me.
You may uncover something deep and difficult to express, and
you may uncover an implied philosophy, psychology or theology which is less than what it seems to be. You may come up
with something new and meaningful. Pay attention to your
response to what others find meaningful.*

ARCHETYPE & ARCHETYPAL IMAGES

When thinking of the word term "image," it is most likely we think of a flat, two-dimensional representation. Our picture of image is determined by common everyday experiences. We see images on television, cell phones, in newspapers, magazines and photo albums. Each of these images contain some form of personal meaning. Each of these images is flat, missing a certain depth because they lack dimension. To look at oneself is not the same visual experience as looking at a picture of oneself. The images we see in our imagination are more than two-dimensional, fluid, full of depth and meaning. These images come to life and live within us through our personal and collective experiences. The challenge explored here is the relationship of image to soul. Soul may be my primary formative image, soul may be imagining me, but what are the images that live within my soul?

Working 'it' out, paying attention to 'it', and being in-tune with whatever 'it' is, satisfies a desire, a need, a longing to learn, to discover, to find, to see.

To see in a way that wants to be seen. To see in a way that is a way of seeing. To see in a way that simply is a way. A way to see. A way to see images. Images of myself, images of others, images of what is happening, images of images.

A way of seeing images containing a feeling of what is sensible. Sensible in that I can see, feel and interact with images through my experience and my perspective. Sensible in how the images begin to take form. Sensible in how the images begin to fit together into larger and larger images.

This fitting and knitting together of images requires the slow removal of the discreetness in distinction of the individual image pieces. The slow removal of the discreetness in distinction begins to fit the image pieces together into larger images.

Larger pieces of the overall image, once created and discovered can have their own meaning. A larger image and associated meaning may be imagined as being an image of an archetype. The archetype itself also can become a subset of the primary personal image, which is being worked out and created through me.

Archetype and archetypal images as a subset of the primary image being worked out through me, and that I am working out. Archetype and archetypal images as a subset of the primary image that moves me, and that I am both creating and discovering, within each iteration of imagination.

In my search for meaning I enjoy reading. I can read about some historically important author, and even read the works of that author. Some concepts, such as archetypes, seem to have a common sense meaning, quickly grasped. The same concept may appear to be more mysterious and even more confusing the further one reads. One day I even decided to write something about archetype which seems to me to be my own idea, and something of a challenge to whatever I have read about archetypes. I do not believe I understand what archetype means. I imagine it to mean something both more and different than what I have read. Archetype is a word that fascinates me, capturing something of my imagination. As such archetype is a meaningful word for me. There is a wealth of meaning inside of what fascinates you and captures your imagination. Such things have a hold on you. You are not alone.

DISTILLING SOMETHING DIVINE
FROM COARSE MATTER

Whether I see myself as on a personal journey or as within an iteration of psyche I am in the process of moving from where I am now to some other place. Certainly it will be the next place, which offers me a better sense of home and soul satisfaction. But soul is not easily satisfied. I will journey from place to place searching for some sense of what seems to be calling out to me and resonating within my bones. I am not satisfied with here but I cannot tell you where satisfaction can be found. It always seems to be just around the corner a millimeter out of my peripheral vision. I may decide to use new tools in my search such as distillation. Heating things up, separating out component parts, intermixing the parts, and looking for essence of me. I may travel far and wide in my search. Rather than find what I am looking for, instead what I may uncover is an important place of perspective.

Let it out. Let it go. Finish the process of distilling some-thing divine from coarse matter. The gods may be around us, their effect felt within us, but to find the gods within us, those voices that live within, may require a slow digestion, a chemical recombination of all that already is and always has been. That which has an invisible, felt shape and form can be too definite and not easily distilled, or boiled, until a vaporous and spir-it-like substance is released then intensified and condensed into another specific shape and form. To find and enjoy something of the spirit is a wonderful by-product of this distillation pro-cess. But this vaporous and spirit-like substance cannot handle the heat of attention. It changes state, disappears and burns off when the heat is on. What remains after the distillation may be what is most valuable, the thick, dense, dark, tactile, shadowy, muck of distillation and refinement.

The gods may be alive within us, yet the specific shape and form of the gods who live in the solar plexus, and the gods who live throughout all our experience, require a refinement of familiarity. We may speak of the gods as archetypes, myths or as fantasy. The general form and effect of an archetype can have something of an unconscious, impersonal, and unrefined existence. Content to be wherever and however it is being ex-pressed. The concept of archetype itself may contain the latent element of fire, or better, the flame and flicker of distillation. At some point in daily life, the flame of refinement, the flame of distillation, the flame that removes what is no longer required, the flame that releases that which wants out, the flame that seizes ones attention, the flame that burns off all that cannot withstand the heat of attention, comes to life and becomes active. A certain combination of elements and conditions sparks the flame of distillation to burn. Something within personal experience sparks the flame of distillation, which distills something of the divine, of the invisible, from visible coarse matter. In this sense, the divine does not distill itself. Rather the divine may be said to be acted upon by some other force, agent, or experience, and in some proper measure, begins to be distilled.

The working assumption here is that there is something within ordinary life, something within ordinary matter which appears to be more than only atoms, more than the elementary particles of physics. There is something within a particular construct of matter or expression of elementary atomic forms that contains the essence of what may be imagined as gods, archetypes and, perhaps even the divine. That which is so desperately sought after can also be that which has always been there, since the beginning. The divine may also be considered as an imaginal quality, a felt experience, which is both a psychological and theological reflection upon my own atoms and a psychological and theological reflection upon the experiences that my own coarse matter has within the story I call life. In this sense, the divine is a by-product of the human process of being in relation to self, other, and all that is experienced. In this sense, the divine comes into being as the stuff of daily experience, is boiled, stirred and agitated within the context of one's experience, within the story of I, me and you.

We may imagine the divine as coming into being, being recognised and seeking recognition, through a certain alchemy of life experience. On the other hand, that which seems to be created and forged within the alchemical process, within my life story, can appear to have a more special, meaningful and everlasting quality than the coarse matter to which it owes its beginning and continued existence. This may be imagined as the creation of something eternal out of the temporal. This requires concentrated work, energy and a sustaining story to bring about the transformation. How much of this creation of the eternal from the temporal, how much of this bringing into being is a release from imposed confines? How much of this creation of the eternal from the temporal is the eventual release and appreciation of what already exists, what has always been available. There within me. There around me. There in the beginning and there in the end. One and the same. There in the beginning seeking a certain recognition and expression: I am as you are. Simultaneously the same, yet different.

The words personal, growth and individuation can imply a step-by-step process, an endless incremental process of self-understanding. There seems to be more of an iterative, rather than incremental process at work. An increment will simply add to or remove from what exists, a specific piece following a linear or predictable path. An iteration gathers all the pieces of what has been, including newly uncovered parts, resulting in something which initially appears random. Given enough iterations, the seemingly random path from place to place begins to trace a unique pattern and image. As I piece the images together into a larger figure, my story, the story of me, I sense my personal story is continuously being re-written. Am I the author, story, director and actor? I somehow change after each iterative edit of my personal story. From this it is possible to imagine both me and I as continuously emerging perspectives.

To see through is not the same as to look at. In looking at, I focus attention on a specific experience, person or object and focus my attention on that thing which has captured my attention. How big is it? How did it get there? What is its name? By practicing at seeing through an object or event or experience,

I first recognize that something has captured my attention. For example, I may cast my attention on my feet. Hello feet. And approach my feet as a story, a fantasy, a path to something else and somewhere else. My feet as a story and passageway to something more than what my eyes and attention are focused upon, as something more than parts of my body touching the floor. My feet seem to have a mind of their own, and are willing to take me where the rest of me wants to go, even toward disaster. In sickness and in health, in good times and in bad times, even in death, my feet are with me. My constant companions.

By attempting to see through, there is an effort to push imagination to a place of encounter and reconciliation within a boundary. The imaginal boundary. The place where I can imagine no further. The imaginal boundary is not the end of imagination, rather it is the limit of where imagination may freely wander. A place of wonder, fear and mystery. I have come out to this place and now there is no place left to go. There is nothing before me but a teasing, impenetrable boundary. This far, and no further. This boundary continues to beckon yet offers nothing in return. While up against the imaginal boundary, it can be valuable to look both left and right, and to turn around and look at all that was once behind me. By turning around, I may enjoy the wonder of what has been and see it all again, experience it all at once. By turning around, away from the boundary, all I see and experience is me. All that is part of me, my vast visual landscape, including all my choices, all my personal iterations. The building of me and my story includes all my yes's and no's. By seeking to distill something divine from coarse matter I have somehow decided what to include and what to exclude from me, and my story.

One of the challenges encountered at the imaginal boundary is being out there, at the edge of my known universe. A feeling of having no solid ground on which to stand, a floating and a swimming inside of the ethereal and mythical. An emptiness to the vastness of possibility. Any place can be everyplace without a stable foundation for my feet to call home. As I turn around and take in all that was once behind me, I long for a sense of a place to call home, where I can stand, where my feet can feel at home. Some say home is where the heart is, or home is wherever you are. Yet following what seems to be my heart's desire can move me far from home, placing me on a constant itinerant iterative path, away from a sense of home, toward what seems to be missing, toward what seems to be calling my soul in a constant, particular direction. What I am called to over there, out there, may be a crucial missing piece of me and my story. What is over there, out there, may more simply be something that must be experienced, and even more so, something which seeks acknowledgment. Only then will it cease calling and reverberating within my soul. That which demands attention commands the satisfaction of recognition. That which calls me may not be a missing piece. It may be that the location of this piece is a perspective. There is nothing here for me to pick up and distill, or to conjoin. This place is not a road sign or a signpost pointing to a specific direction. This is a place to stand. This is a place of vision, recall and appreciation.

As I turn around at the imaginal boundary and see all that was once behind me, and as I long for a sense of home, what I see is home stretched out before me. Home. Home is where I have already been. Home is territory which has already been explored. My story is my home. It may be I cannot find, enjoy and appreciate the stable, familiar ground of home until the in-search and the out-search of unfamiliar and ungrounded places has been satisfied. Rather than end up at a place of no return, I arrive at a place of being able to begin to return. A return towards an enjoyment and thankfulness for where I am now. A return towards a sense of who I am now. A return towards an experience of being lived within. An increased trust in my personal iterative process. A place of grace, gratitude, grounding and meaning. A place always available under these restless feet.

Searching for meaning may include seeking something of the divine. In using the word divine, I search for a word, a relationship with the feeling that it is more than me. I am having an experience, a thought, a feeling, and some of these seem to originate from outside of me. They are happening within me, yet it can feel as if I am not the source. These can be welcome experiences but where is their source? There can be the feeling that there is more to me, more to you, more to the world and more to the universe than atoms and elementary particles of physics. I may spend some time, or part of my entire life seeking this source. If I find the source, this mysterious invisible other, then surely I will uncover something meaningful. Seeking this source, the divine, can feed and occupy my imagination, and even my spare time. If I have taken time to free myself from the hold the economy has on my soul, and focus on finding the invisible, have I not simply replaced one tormentor of the soul with another? On the other hand there may be something within me, something within my soul not easily satisfied. The restless companion of the human condition will continue to speak to me and move me in a particular direction until it gains some satisfaction. Soul satisfaction. The experience of something and someone as the other within me could also be imagined as my soul. My restless soul moving me towards a place where we will both find home, satisfaction and meaning. Home can be about my physical location, the people and places within my life. Home can also be related to perspective, how I see myself, all that is and has been a part of my life. Home is where I am and where I have been. My personal story is my home. While at home I also continue to follow myself home. Home is where my center of gravity of being resides. I feel at home when I have the experience of being lived within.

I AM
NOT INVISIBLE

I was having difficulty putting into words the thoughts, feelings, and images of Mike the factory floor worker, discussed below. I thought rationally about his situation and analyzed the relevant information. Yet the words would not flow. My initial perspective had, in effect silenced Mike and rendered him invisible. My analysis of Mike had blinded me to his soul. With a change in perspective, imagining myself beyond being in Mike's shoes, as Mike on the factory floor, both Mike and what he had to say became visible. I allowed Mike and his soul to speak through me.

This discussion relates to the past, the present, and what might be the future of life within capitalism. This discussion relates to the effect of capitalism on the collective human experience, including the effect of capitalism on the individual. It is possible to speak of a collective effect of capitalism on the human condition. Speaking of a collective effect begins to approach speaking about an abstraction, a statistical summary, something imagined, something invisible. Who, what and where are the visible people and places, when gathered together into a collective, become invisible as a statistic? Rather than gaining some sense of meaning through this collective, any sense of individual meaning seems to be statistically smoothed out. Each individual person is transformed into a probability distribution.

The context of the past, presented here, concerns a factory floor worker in the 1920's. The industrial revolution was fully entwined into everyday life. Capitalism and a consumer society were a rock-solid part of the daily routine. Yet, there was a significant gap between the rich and the poor. In the 1920's, communism became one political option not only for the poor, but for those who embraced a philosophy of wealth sharing, "we and ours," versus the capitalistic concentration of wealth, "me and mine." The poor worked long hours, long days and long weeks to provide food, clothing and shelter for themselves and their families. Working conditions were often miserable, and workers began to form unions and to strike for better wages, improved workplace conditions, and shorter work days. Through this struggle, there emerged a middle class and the foundation of our current work environment. And yet, the gap between the wealthy and the poor again widens as the middle class contracts, with much of the middle class subsumed into the category of working poor. In today's parlance, we might speak of this economic disparity as a tension between the 99% and the 1%. Within this framework, there is the sense that what occurred one hundred years ago is happening again. One hundred years ago workers felt invisible, but then great masses of working poor began to rise up and become visible.

One hundred years ago it was much more common for Protestants and Catholics to be active members of a church and support church activities. With the rise of capitalism and long hours in poor working conditions, many people stopped attending church activities. The Catholic Church launched a rather innovative response, "worker priests," evangelizing downtrodden factory workers in order to solicit their return to the church. These priests worked side-by-side on the factory floor, spoke to workers about church, enjoining them to return back to church and to the Church. What follows is a response by a 1920's factory floor worker. As a member of the working class, part of a huge collective, this worker sought recognition, meaning, and visibility. His words continue to resonate today:

"Hi my name is Mike. I am Michael's proletariat worker persona. Michael, a decent man, whom I continue to converse with, who gives of his time and money to assist the working class, who shares memories of the daily struggle of life on the factory floor, has become part of the elite, living up in the air, in a condo, overlooking the lake. Michael has asked me, his alter-ego from the past, to write this passage, as he no longer is one of us, no longer carrying a "worn to the bone feeling," that slowly being ground into dust by the daily grind feeling. The daily grind. The daily grind. This is my world without end. Amen.

I call my fellow workers "comrades." In doing so I do not profess myself as a communist. Instead it is an identification, a solidarity with my coworkers, the ones with whom I go into battle every day on the factory floor. Together we combat fatigue, poor working conditions, and united we face the daily grind. Together we face the supreme challenge of making it through one more day. Today, we battle for today. To make it to the final whistle blow. Our battle is to provide food, clothing and shelter for our wives and children. It is safe to say that we do not have the slightest interest in the beyond, in the invisible. I become fatigued simply imagining tomorrow.

Perhaps you cannot comprehend the full impact capitalism has on me. I fight for a decent life within capitalism every day. From your elite position you may see capitalism as the lesser of two evils, yet from my perspective, from where I stand every day, capitalism is the enemy while socialism is the lesser of two evils. I have been observing the priest who has come to work with us with interest; he is struggling to adapt to our work environment. He is beginning to understand my lack of interest in the invisible actually results from the fact that my entire focus is on the present, on today. I cannot afford an elitist luxury of relaxation and reflection. If I ever stop to relax I fear I may not be able to ever start moving again.

What is also interesting to me is that your church has discovered that factory work is overwhelming for your worker priests. They are not able to maintain a proper spiritual life once the daily grind has worn them to the bone. So of what value is your church to me, of what value is this spirituality to me, of what value is any concept regarding the beyond, the invisible, even as your trained representative is overwhelmed by the daily grind? Your priest has become our comrade. There is something more which sustains him. This interests me. I begin to see that I cannot live by bread alone, but it is important for you to know that I also cannot live without bread. This is my supreme priority.

As I see the positive effect of your spirituality on you, within my context, I begin to have a direct experience of the invisible supporting you. I might see the invisible in you. Your uniform does carry a certain persona: I am a priest. I may simply respond to your uniform. The name of your profession, ie: priest, also symbolizes a certain persona. Yet it is easier for me to talk to the man, ie: the priest, without the distraction of the uniform. The invisible power within who you are, ie: priest, is more important to me.

If you talk to me only to tell me your story, how long will I listen? If you listen to my story solely to tell me your story, I will smell a rat and shut down. How can you genuinely listen to my story and in so doing help me to see where I am, what I want and perhaps even a flicker of this invisible which is yearning to be fanned into flame.

I can have the experience of something invisible at work within me and even living within me. I can also have the experience of being invisible, or feeling as if I am invisible. Who notices me? Does anyone care that I have certain feelings? Am I a cog in a machine? How much do I suffer in silence?

We have been talking to some extent about the invisible as being something within which there can be meaning. Feeling invisible is the other side of the coin, the other side of invisible. To feel invisible can bring a sense of nothingness, of meaninglessness. This is a difficult place to be and a complicated place to stand. While on the factory floor, Mike found something of his voice. He had something to say. In saying something to someone he became visible, both to the listener and also to himself. He began talking about them: the priest and the Catholic Church. He finished by talking about himself, and his own flicker of the invisible. Within the conversation between self and other, in seeking to be heard in some way, there can be meaning. Here is where meaning can be both created and discovered at the same time.

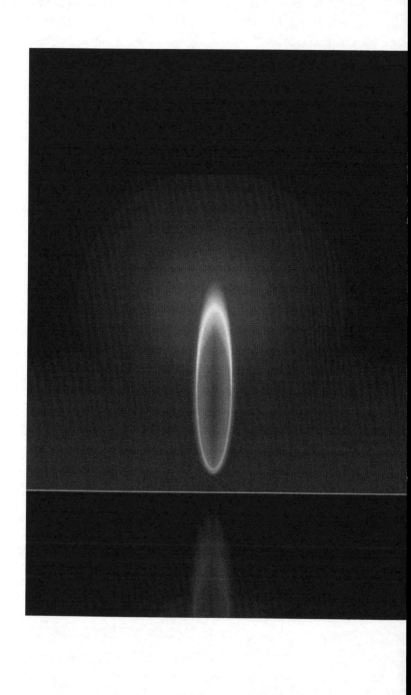

A FLICKER
OF THE INVISIBLE

What is the point of demarcation between the visible and the invisible? It would seem that materialism has shaped our current notion that seeing is believing. What I see and measure is visible and what I cannot see and measure may be said to be more than invisible, it does not exist. What has and is lost is the appreciation and acceptance of a felt sense of experience. I can feel love, but can I measure love? I may be able to measure the effect of love but this is not a measure of the cause, love itself. Does this mean that love is invisible or a figment of the imagination? The same can be asked about God and archetypes. I may not be able to visually see either one but I can experience both. What is the value of my personal experience in determining what is real, be it visible to my eyes, or invisible to my eyes, but felt within my body and soul.

A flicker of the invisible. A fanning into flame a flicker of the invisible. There is something or someone moving within experience, within phenomena, which can be named as invisible. Some may say God or a god is invisible. Some may say an archetype is invisible. Both can be seen indirectly through their manifestation within the collective and within the individual. In naming a manifestation of the invisible as God or a god or as an archetype, are we simply naming an effect and are not naming the thing or the being itself? We give a name to the effect of the invisible. We have named a relational phenomenon. A phenomenon we see as having some direct connection with the invisible. We posit an invisible. Then the concept of the invisible is taken one step further by positing a name for what seems to be invisible. The invisible as a God or a god or an archetype or some other mysterious universal life force.

What is gained by seeking to further name and qualify that which is so hard to grasp, not only because it is invisible, but because it does not seem to have a direct form, it seems to be recognized only by its experiential effect rather than its direct appearance. The invisible remains as already and not yet. The invisible remains imperceptible, experienced within phenomenon yet somehow devoid of any distinct personal manifestation. When encountering what could be called the invisible do we encounter something completely other, with being, form and shape, which simply exists in such a way as to be experienced

yet always invisible? When encountering what could be called
the invisible, do we meet something inherently visible yet rendered invisible through our perspective?

Something or someone remains invisible as it remains
out of sight, out on the edge of imagination. Yet the invisible
is not hiding. It is our perspective, our way of seeing, which
has become unable to perceive directly or by effect what and
who is right there, what and who has always been available.
The mystery of the invisible is not some quality of the invisible. The mystery shrouding the invisible is the veil of perspective, both collective and personal. The veil of perspective
shrouds the ability to see and to experience what and who has
been with us at all time.

*In writing specifically about the invisible I am also writing
about meaning. There is something or someone moving within
experience, within phenomena, which can be called meaningful. In saying that something has meaning, or is meaningful,
we have named a relational phenomenon. Meaning does not
stand on its own. Meaning is found within relationship, in relation to something or someone. Something or someone remains
meaningless if out of sight, out of vision, out on the edges of
imagination. Meaning is not hiding. It is our perspective, our*

way of seeing which renders as invisible what and who is right there, what and who has always been available.

The mystery of meaning is not some quality of meaning. The mystery which shrouds meaning is the veil of perspective, both collective and personal, which shrouds the ability to see and to experience what and who has been with us at all time.

JUST
IMAGINE

I have been fascinated by dreams for as long as I can recall. My first ever science project in grade 7 was on dreams. If one was to sleep eight hours a night until age 60 one would have slept 20 years. The body rests and regenerates while we sleep. As we slip into that certain unconscious place, we dream. Dreamtime is the place where psyche and soul enjoy freedom of expression and movement. Dreamtime is the place of image, story, messages and play. Some dreams often feel like nothing more than a random collection of nonsense. Other dreams, even dreams within dreams, can have a feeling of great personal importance. This dream is more than the random wanderings of my unconscious. This dream has meaning and more meaning than I will ever consciously understand. Below is one of these dreams.

I had a dream. I was in a setting full of activity.

The commotion of the dream figures focused on cleaning up, renovating, rebuilding an old church and its grounds- like the smaller older churches and yards found in England. I walk into this scene of activity. I am drawn to the front of an old, stone Catholic Church, where a wood crucifix is being attended to. I speak to the workers regarding their labour and they demonstrate how the wood (natural material) is being reinforced by driving metal (synthetic material) through the center of the pieces of wood. The arms, legs and so on. I was interested in this process of restoration, that a process was required, and that the process could be accomplished.

I was saddened that this house of God, the church grounds and the building were falling into a state of disrepair due to age and neglect. The crucifix once hung front and center behind the altar. I went up to the place where the crucifix had been removed, and focused my attention on the location where the crucifix once hung on the wall. With the crucifix removed, two words were semi-transparent on the wall: "Just imagine." Behind and through this symbol there was an entrance, an invitation to a new iteration of perspective.

Dreams are wonderful, frightening, confusing, sad, a strange collection of people and places doing something and having something to say as I sleep. Dreams can be mysterious. A dream may even continue to speak to me after I awaken. I may wake up feeling afraid, sad, loved or amazed, and this feeling may remain all day. What is the meaning of these images, which come to me and have their way within me as I sleep?

I have often wondered about the meaning of dreams. What I have discovered is that no one dream or no one image from a dream has one particular meaning that can be uncovered within a dream dictionary. What I have learned is that this dream is seeking to tell me a story, using words, images and people I recognize in some way. This dream is seeking to say something. As such there can be meaning within the dream. It would seem the meaning of many dreams is shrouded within the mystery of the presentation of the dream. What on earth was that dream about? It is easier to gaze into and through some dreams. Something meaningful can fall out of a dream, as if from nowhere, such as when you are brushing your teeth, standing in the elevator, or out for a walk. There are the dreams which offer sudden and much more immediate insights. Oh my!... this is an important dream. These dreams are filled with the same cast of characters, places, symbols and images as any other dream. Yet there is something different about this dream. Through the dream I see something new, or as if for the first time. Such a dream is a revelation. A new perspective, a new way of imagining, of seeing, where the invisible becomes visible. Through the dream it is as if something meaningful appeared out of nowhere. A flash of unconscious dream insight can bring an important meaning into consciousness. There may even be a dream, which is somehow able to see through itself, through its own symbols and its own images. A dream may somehow use primary symbolic meaningful imagery to see through and into a new meaningful perspective. Here there is a taste of something even more meaningful. A relationship between meanings where each meaning requires the other meaning to be meaningful.

CONCLUSION

The immensity of what is and extent of what is possible can obscure and render opaque any hope of finding something, or someone meaningful. The hectic confines of everyday life can restrict and blur our vision to anything and anyone meaningful. Yet something within us still yearns for meaning. Something within us asks what the meaning of life is, asks what the meaning of my life is. What is this something? Is this my soul? Is this my unconscious? Is this my muse? Is this something of the divine resonating within me? Is this but an echo of the neurons firing in my brain? The answer to these questions influence your perspective of self, other, the world, the universe and even the consciousness asking these questions. The answer to any of these questions will affect the meaning you seek, the meaning you discover, the meaning you make, and the meanings you hold onto through life.

This is a summary of some of the meanings explored here, which might help you within your own process:

1. *Meaninglessness is related to nothingness, sameness, lack of distinction, and lack of differentiation. In recognizing separateness, discreetness, in sticking with the image, in working to create something from what feels like nothing, meaning can begin to be found by being in-relation-to something.*

2. *My center of gravity of being has always been with me and will continue to be with me. Beginning to have an internal sense of both soul and home carries with it a sense of meaning and becomes an internal center of gravity of being towards which all of me gravitates and feels grounded.*

3. *Sometimes within the search for meaning, the focus on the search itself can obscure or obstruct from view anything meaningful. The "full on" search for meaning can unleash a sense of meaninglessness. In looking so very hard for something, I may find nothing.*

4. *Each thing that seeks release may require different vehicles of expression. Each thing that seeks release*

might not fully reveal itself until the end of the process, as if meaning finding expression and the vehicle of expression, and the perseverance to stick with it are all part and parcel of the same package. Over and over again, there is no quick fix or easy way round to find or to express something meaningful. There is simply trust and persistence of soul, the restless companion of the human condition.

5. *The barriers into meaning can be both collective and personal. The collective barriers can be most harmful when they remain invisible.*

6. *The rattle in our shadow and the rattle in your soul can be meaningful, vibrating us to attention, attuning us to all of who we always have been.*

7. *What is left behind within each personal iteration, either consciously or unconsciously, begins to dampen and cast a shadow upon any discovery of wellbeing and meaning being found. I can frustrate my own sense of wellbeing, my own sense of meaning, through the process I employ to adapt to personal change. You will not need to look long and hard to find your 'shit', your 'shit' will find you.*

8. *Within Teilhard de Chardin's personal theological struggle and search for meaning, the universe itself becomes meaningful, with a direction and purpose. Imagine that. The personal meaning I uncover may be greater than myself and my life, and helpful to others during their search for meaning.*

9. *Pay attention to your response to what others find meaningful. You may uncover something deep and difficult to express, and you may uncover an implied philosophy or psychology or theology, which is less than what it seems to be. You may come up with something new and meaningful for you.*

10. *There is a wealth of meaning inside what fascinates and captures your imagination. Such things have a hold on you. You are not alone.*

11. *Rather than winding up at a point of no return, one ends up at a place where one can begin to return. A return to enjoyment and gratitude for where I am now. A return towards a sense of who I am now. A return towards an experience of being lived within. This is a place of grace, gratitude, grounding and*

meaning. This is a place that has always been available under those restless feet.

12. *Feeling invisible is the other side of the coin, the other side of invisible. Within the conversation between self and other, seeking to be heard in some way, there can be meaning. Here is where meaning can be both created and discovered at the same time.*

13. *The mystery of meaning is not some quality of meaning. The mystery shrouding meaning is the veil of perspective, both collective and personal, cloaking the ability to see and experience what and who has been with us all along.*

14. *There can exist a relationship between meanings where each meaning requires the other meaning to be meaningful.*

15. *Something meaningful may be happening even when we do not see any meaning. How can we also begin to see, feel or begin to trust that something meaningful is happening at any given moment, even if this meaning is not felt and visible?*

What is the meaning of life? In seeking answers, I have never been comfortable with the specific phrasing of this question. This inquiry prompts one to imagine and to seek after 'the meaning,' as in the 'one meaning', the only true and objective meaning, which somehow is out there on its own, waiting to be discovered. As previously noted, meaning does not stand on its own. Meaning is found within relationships, in relation to something or someone. Something or someone remains meaningless as it remains out of sight, out of vision, out on the invisible edges of imagination. Meaning is not hiding. It is our perspective which seems to render imperceptible, what and who is right here, what and who has always been available. The mystery of meaning is not some quality of meaning. The mystery which shrouds meaning is the veil of perspective, both collective and personal. In this context it might be better to ask: what meanings within my life can be discovered, made and treasured? What meanings do I seek and what meanings seek me? I enjoy these questions. It is entirely possible that the meaning you seek is with you right now, providing the solid ground for your restless soul.

Made in the USA
Charleston, SC
26 June 2015